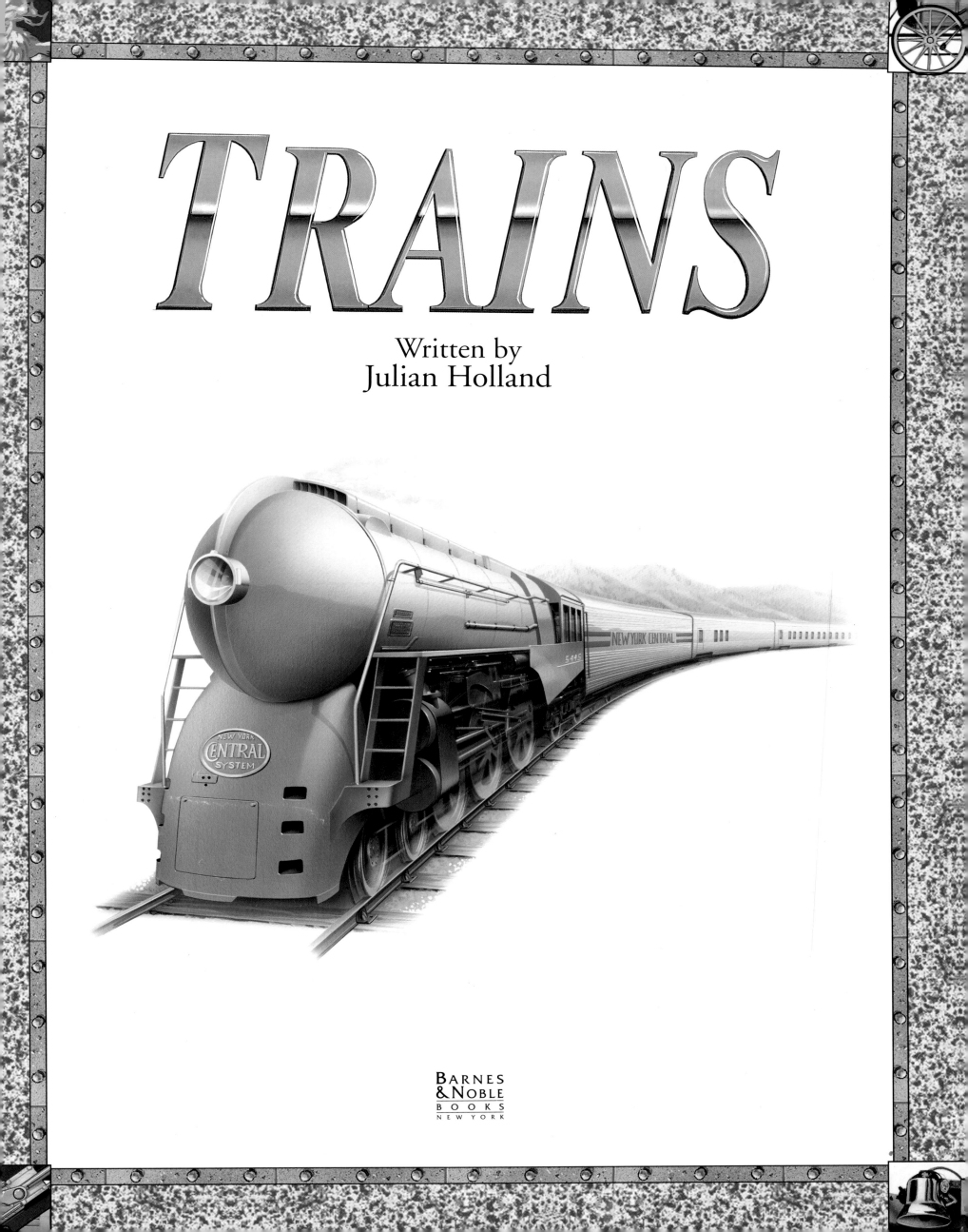

TRAINS

Written by
Julian Holland

BARNES
&NOBLE
BOOKS
NEW YORK

ACKNOWLEDGMENTS

Illustrated by
Julian Baker, Chris Brown, Peter Bull, Bob Corley
(Artist Partners), Anthony Cowland, Robert Farnworth,
Terry Hadler (Bernard Thornton Artists), Nick
Hawker, Paul Higgens (Ian Fleming & Associates),
Ray Hutchins, Julia Osorno, Roger Payne (Linden
Artists) Steve Seymour (Bernard Thornton Artists),
Alan Weston (Linden Artists), Gerald Whitcomb
(Specs Art), Sean Wilkinson

Picture credits
14 (top left) Venice-Simplon Orient Express Ltd,
23 (top left), 23 (bottom right) London Regional
Transport Contract 96-2409 Registered user

*The Publishers would also like to thank the following for
their assistance*
London Transport Museum
Venice-Simplon Orient Express Ltd
The Puffing Billy Railway Information Service

This edition published by
Barnes & Noble, Inc., by arrangement with
Andromeda Oxford Limited

1996 Barnes & Noble Books

Planned and produced by
Andromeda Oxford Limited
11–15 The Vineyard
Abingdon
Oxon OX14 3PX

Copyright © Andromeda Oxford Limited 1996

Reprinted 1998

ISBN 0-7607-0289-6 Trains
M 10 9 8 7 6 5 4 3 2

Printed in Italy

DOMINION OF NEW ZEALAND

Streamlined designs were introduced in the 1930s to improve aerodynamics, making trains look sleek and fast. However, the streamlined covers had to be removed for maintenance work. This Class A4 4-6-2 locomotive, *Dominion of New Zealand*, is identical to *Mallard*, which set the world speed record for steam in 1938 at 126 miles (202.7 kilometers) per hour.

Dominion of New Zealand
1930s, steam
6 driving wheels
90mph (160kph)

TGV ATLANTIQUE

The current world rail speed record was set on May 18, 1990, by a specially modified French TGV Atlantique electric train. The TGV accelerated to 319 miles (515 kilometers) per hour on the new high-speed line from Le Mans to Tours. TGVs in daily service on new high-speed lines in France regularly reach speeds of up to 186 miles (300 kilometers) per hour.

TGV Atlantique
Electric, 1980s
8 driving wheels (each end)
319mph (515kph; world record set in 1990)

Maglev train
A.D. 2045?
No wheels
496mph (800kph)

TRANSRAPID 06

Trains for the future are being designed without wheels, making them even faster. Prototypes of these "maglev" trains have been built already in Germany and Japan. Maglev trains use the principle of magnetic levitation, almost eliminating friction. Magnetic forces are able to propel the train at great speed. These high-speed trains will be ideal for long-distance travel, at speeds of up to 496 miles (800 kilometers) per hour.

1879: DC electric motor invented in Germany, making electric trains possible.

1881: First public electric railroad opens near Berlin, Germany.

1890: First electric underground train opens in London.

1938: *Mallard* sets the world steam speed record of 126 miles (202.7 kilometers) per hour.

1940s: Diesel locomotives begin to replace steam. They could travel longer distances in less time because they did not need to stop so often for refueling. The first diesel locomotive was built in Germany in 1913.

1941: Big Boy, the largest steam locomotive ever built, is produced in the United States for the Union Pacific Railroad.

1964: The first monorail line opens in Tokyo.

1994: The Channel Tunnel for trains between England and France opens.

1996: Maglev train opens at Disney World in Florida, running at 248 miles (400 kilometers) per hour.

Rocket

PASSENGER COMFORT

First-class passenger coaches built for the Liverpool and Manchester Railway in 1830 were similar to stagecoaches. Although their design was simple compared with modern coaches, they had sprung buffers to absorb impact. The brakeman sat on the roof where passengers kept their luggage. Until 1844, third-class passengers traveled in coaches without a roof.

The *Rocket* was designed and built by George and Robert Stephenson. It was the first intercity steam locomotive, and it ran between Liverpool and Manchester. But it became well known for another reason. In 1829 a contest was held to find the best locomotive to run on George Stephenson's new Liverpool and Manchester Railway. *Rocket* was the only locomotive that was able to do everything that was required in the contest, and it was awarded the prize. It reached a speed of 29 miles (46.6 kilometers) per hour with a full load, and it was able to haul coachloads of passengers at 20 miles (32 kilometers) per hour up a steep slope. *Rocket's* success was helped by some special technical features. These were a multitubed boiler that made steam quickly; tilting cylinders that powered the driving wheels using a connecting rod; a blast pipe that created a better draft for the fire by sending steam exhaust up the chimney; and a separate firebox covered by a water-jacket. Although many other steam trains were copied from *Rocket's* basic design, *Rocket* itself was soon replaced on the railroad by an improved model called the *Planet* – also designed by the Stephensons – which gave a smoother ride.

Chimney

Steam dome

Boiler

Water tank

Tender

Connecting rod

Driving wheel

CHANGING GAUGES

The broad-gauge track of the GWR caused problems because it was wider than the standard railroad track used in the rest of Britain. The task of changing the GWR to the standard gauge began in 1869, after a Royal Commission ruled that the broad gauge must go. In May 1892, the conversion was finally finished using an army of over 4,000 men.

Smokebox
With blast pipe inside.

Boiler tubes
Multi-tubed boiler produced higher steam pressure.

Handbrake
With control handle.

Leaf springs
Provided basic suspension.

Internal cylinder
Transfered power to a single pair of very large driving wheels.

Bogie
Leading fixed 4-wheel bogie.

Driving wheel
8ft. (2.4m) diameter driving wheel.

Bogie
Trailing fixed 2-wheel bogie.

Wooden brake blocks
Often caught fire due to heat of friction.

Although weighing nearly 40 tons and measuring 45ft. (13.64m) long, the *Lord of the Isles* had only two driving wheels, measuring 8ft. (2.4m) in diameter, and one set of brakes with wooden brake blocks.

ISAMBARD KINGDOM BRUNEL (1806–1859)

Brunel was the engineer of the Great Western Railway from 1833 until his death, and designed the broad-gauge London–Bristol line. Although some of his early projects failed, his finest achievements include the Clifton Suspension Bridge and the steamships *Great Western* and *Great Britain*.

Chimney

Outer frame

Smokebox

THE CREW

The driver and fireman of the *Lord of the Isles* worked in an open-air cab. They needed to be hardy: The cab's small side-sheets and "spectacles," fitted on the backplate, gave them little shelter as they traveled at 60 miles (96 kilometers) per hour, sometimes through driving wind and rain. But on hot days there was no way to get away from the heat of the boiler.

11

T he General

Promontory Point

0   1,600 km

"The train toiled over this infinity like a snail; and being the one thing moving, it was wonderful what huge proportions it began to assume in our regard. It seemed miles in length, and either end of it within but a step of the horizon."
Robert Louis Stevenson, *Emigrant Train*

The first North American steam-operated railroad opened in 1830 and by 1855 nearly 21,960 miles (35,420 kilometers) of track had been laid. Because of its ability to give a smoother ride on the roughly laid tracks, the 4-4-0 type of steam locomotive rapidly became the standard American locomotive used on nearly every railroad. The *General* was a typical wood-burning 4-4-0 locomotive of this period. Wood was used as fuel because this was more plentiful than coal in the Midwest. A large spark arrester was fitted to the chimney to help eliminate forest and grassland fires along the track. A massive cowcatcher was fitted at the front to provide protection on the unfenced lines. During the Civil War, from 1861 to 1865, when large armies and supplies were moved by rail, the *General* became famous as a victim of kidnapping. Union soldiers captured the *General*, a Confederate locomotive, between Atlanta and Chattanooga. Hotly pursued for nearly 90 miles (145 kilometers) by another Confederate locomotive, *Texas*, the *General* eventually ran out of fuel. The kidnappers were hanged as spies.

LINKING THE OCEANS

During the Civil War, Abraham Lincoln authorized the first railway across the United States. Two railroad companies, the Central Pacific from the West and the Union Pacific from the East, eventually linked up at Promontory Point in Utah on May 10, 1869.

Spark arrester

Bell

Chimney

FUELING THE *GENERAL*

Logs, cut from nearby forests, were loaded into the locomotive tender for fuel. Water for the boiler was fed by hose from water towers into large tanks, also contained in the tender. Sand, which enabled the locomotive to grip slippery rails, was stored in a huge dome on the top of the boiler.

Cowcatcher

Boiler
Turned water into steam.

Cab
Gave protection to driver and fireman.

Spark
chim
Rec
ris
f

Firebox
Logs were burned inside to heat the water.

Tender
Eight-wheeled double bogie.

The *General* was a wood-bu
of the American standard t
engine weighed 26.3 tons.
speeds of up to 60mph (9

Sand storage dome

eeling–Himalayan
press

*"Up the hill goes the narrow-gauge train from Darjeeling to Ghoom,
and down the road comes Asia on foot."*
Peter Allen, *On the Old Lines*

he Darjeeling–Himalayan Railway climbs more than 6,000 feet (1,829 meters) up
he steep slopes of the Himalayas. Opened in 1881, it was engineered by Franklin
e of the East Bengal Railway and was designed to follow the winding course of
army road. It runs for 51 miles (82 kilometers) from the plains at Siliguri to the
s of the Himalayas at Darjeeling. The main climb of 16 miles (25.75
rs) has a steep gradient averaging 1-in-29. To climb the slopes, switchbacks
re used instead of expensive tunnels and bridges. The first locomotives used
ere eight small British 0-4-0 tank engines. Their short wheel base
to ride along the tightly curving narrow-gauge track. By 1927, 32
ves of this type had been built. Some of them are still in use,
they can haul loads of up to 50 tons up a steep slope. The
oldest surviving example now operates at the
Railway Transport Museum, New
Delhi, India.

Coal
bunker

Guard rail
to protect
sanding crew

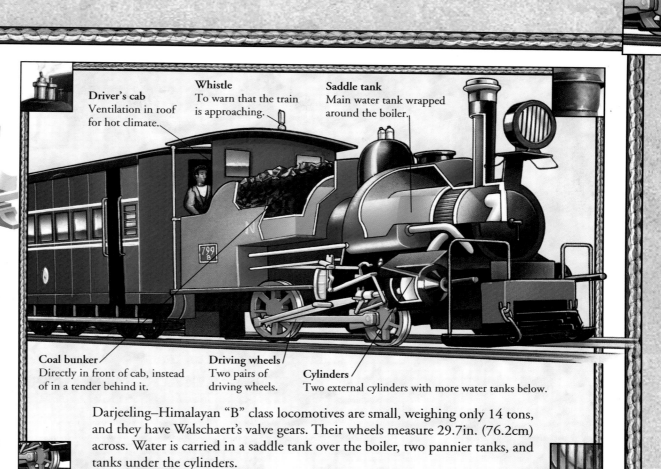

Driver's cab
Ventilation in roof for hot climate.

Whistle
To warn that the train is approaching.

Saddle tank
Main water tank wrapped around the boiler.

Coal bunker
Directly in front of cab, instead of in a tender behind it.

Driving wheels
Two pairs of driving wheels.

Cylinders
Two external cylinders with more water tanks below.

Darjeeling–Himalayan "B" class locomotives are small, weighing only 14 tons, and they have Walschaert's valve gears. Their wheels measure 29.7in. (76.2cm) across. Water is carried in a saddle tank over the boiler, two pannier tanks, and tanks under the cylinders.

125 inches (300 centi-
n a short time. Sand is
help the locomotive's
ls. Most modern trains
oment, but the
an engines also have a
sander who perches on
front of the locomotive
dropping sand on the
rails as the train moves
slowly forward.

GETTING A FREE RIDE

Rail travel is popular in India and trains can be very crowded. When there is no more room in the compartments – or to avoid paying the fare – some passengers cling to the roof or sides of the coach even though this is very dangerous. The roof is also used to stow baggage when the carriages become too crowded. The narrow-gauge Darjeeling–Himalayan train is so slow that passengers can leap off when the train is entering a loop and jump on again when it reaches the other side.

Narrow-gauge passenger coach

LOOPS AND SWITCHBACKS

Two ways in which railroads can scale heights are by using loops and switchbacks. In a loop (above), the line spirals until it crosses over itself. On the Darjeeling–Himalayan Railway, a loop at Batasia makes two spirals to take the train 140 feet (42.67 meters) higher. In a switchback (right), a train drives into a dead end and backs uphill into a second dead end before going forward up the mountain.

Orient-Exp

"[For the first journey in 1883] Nagelmackers had spared no effort to ensure the success of this much-publicized trip, providing beautiful crystal and linen, elaborate food, exclusive wine and impeccable service."
Shirley Sherwood, *The Venice Simplon Orient-Express*

The famous Orient-Express made its first run from Paris to (now Istanbul) in 1883. It was run by a Belgian company Nagelmackers. The train was the height of luxury and its lavish based on American Pullmans. Crossing seven countries, its jour (2,988 kilometers) took 67.5 hours. After the Simplon Tunnel Italy and Switzerland, the train was relaunched as the Simplon 1919. Starting in Calais, France, it made journeys to Istanbul, Bucharest. By 1930, it had linked up with the Taurus Express, in Egypt. By 1932, services also ran from Berlin, Ostend, Ams Prague. The Simplon Orient-Express did not run during Worla withdrawn in 1977. But in 1982, with restored Pullman and Wagons carriages, it was launched as the Venice Simplon Orient-Express. The new service runs between London and Venice.

THE ORIENT-EXPRESS AS POPULAR CULTURE

This poster of the Orient Express is drawn in the Art Deco style in which the train was decorated in the 1930s. The Orient-Express has also starred in many books and movies. The most famous is Agatha Christie's *Murder on the Orient-Express*, filmed in 1974.

VENICE SIMPLON
ORIENT-EXPRESS
LONDON · PARIS · VENICE

Official passenger list

Dining car

COMPAGNIE INTERNATIONALE DES WAGONS-LITS ET DES GRANDS EXPRESS EUROPEENS

Porter

Nº 3541

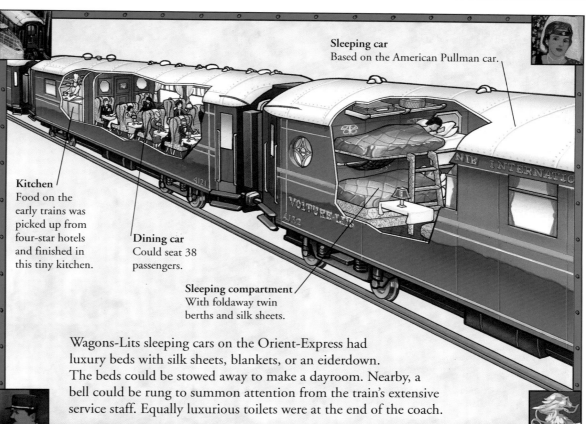

Sleeping car
Based on the American Pullman car.

Kitchen
Food on the early trains was picked up from four-star hotels and finished in this tiny kitchen.

Dining car
Could seat 38 passengers.

Sleeping compartment
With foldaway twin berths and silk sheets.

Wagons-Lits sleeping cars on the Orient-Express had luxury beds with silk sheets, blankets, or an eiderdown. The beds could be stowed away to make a dayroom. Nearby, a bell could be rung to summon attention from the train's extensive service staff. Equally luxurious toilets were at the end of the coach.

THE WAGONS-LITS COMPANY

Impressed by Pullman sleeping cars, the Belgian Georges Nagelmackers built the first European sleeping cars. He founded the Compagnie Internationale des Wagons-Lits (International Sleeping Car Company), which still exists today. This was the company that launched the Orient-Express in 1883. Its distinctive blue and gold logo adorned the original carriages and is used on the modern cars.

Locomotive

BOAT TRAIN

The Wagons-Lits sleeping compartments of the trains that crossed the English Channel – on the way from London to Paris – had to transfer to a boat. Carriage by carriage, the train was loaded onto large ferries to make the crossings.

LONDON TO CAIRO BY TRAIN

In 1930, the journey from London (1) to Cairo (5) by rail took seven days. Passengers crossed by ferry to Calais (2) to board the Simplon Orient-Express. It went as far as Istanbul (3), but passengers could take connecting lines as far as Baghdad (4) and Cairo. The train that went to Cairo was called the Taurus Express. Passengers had to get off the train and take a bus through much of Palestine, where there were no railroads.

DINING ON THE ORIENT-EXPRESS

Food for the meals originally came from four-star hotels in Paris, with fresh supplies picked up from stations during the journey. The size of the kitchen has grown with each new version of the train. Today's Venice Simplon Orient-Express has eight chefs and four dishwashers. Passengers have always dined in luxury, with rich menus and fine wines to choose from. The waiters on the original train wore powdered wigs, waistcoats and silk stockings. The dining cars of the 1930s were decorated with Art Deco designs by famous European artists.

Twentieth Century Ltd

"At the zenith of steam operation in the United States, busiest among the great trunk routes were the rivals operating between New York and Chicago. The two world-famous trains were the Twentieth Century Limited and the Broadway Limited, with average speeds of 58mph {93kph}."

O. S. Nock, *World Atlas of Railways*

In 1902, the New York Central Railroad introduced the Twentieth Century Limited express to Chicago — then the second-largest city in the United States. By 1932 the train had become so popular that it had to be run in three separate sections, each with 13 cars. They left New York's Grand Central Station simultaneously at 2:45p.m. for the 20-hour journey. Electric haulage was used for the first 32 miles (51 kilometers) from New York to Harmon, where a Hudson 4-6-4 steam locomotive took over. Faster trains reduced the journey to 18 hours in 1932, and to 16 hours in 1938, when stream-lined locomotives were introduced. The Twentieth Century Limited was very smart in appearance. It had a club and baggage car containing a bathroom, a barber's shop, a steward's pantry and a smoking lounge; nine sleeping cars; two dining cars; and an observation car. It had its own phone system and secretarial service. First-class passengers traveled in private luxury suites. Diesel locomotives were used after World War 2 until the service was stopped in 1967.

GRAND CENTRAL STATION, NEW YORK CITY

Passengers boarding the Twentieth Century Limited walked along a 259-foot-long (79-meter-long) maroon carpet laid out on the platform at Grand Central Station. This famous station has a cathedral-like concourse that is overlooked by the rococo-style Golden Clock, complete with a draped figure of Mercury and the American eagle. Under the clock was a favorite meeting place for people in New York. The station is now dwarfed by skyscrapers.

Streamlined nose covering smokebox

Handrail

Inspection cover

NEW YORK CENTRAL SYSTEM

1

2

3

STREAMLINING

In the 1930s many railroads introduced streamlined locomotives to reduce wind resistance and make the trains look sleek and fast. The 4-4-2 steam locomotive Hiawatha (1) was introduced in 1935 on the Milwaukee Railroad. The Pennsylvania Railroad introduced this Class T1 4-4-4-4 locomotive (2) in 1942. The Paris-Orleans railroad used 4-6-2 engines like this one (3) built in 1937.

ROUTE OF THE TWENTIETH CENTURY LIMITED

The 955 miles (1,541 kilometers) of the New York Central line followed the Hudson River and was mostly level. Engines and crews were changed at Syracuse and Toledo. Crews were changed also at Albany, Buffalo, Cleveland and Elkhart.

Driving wheels
Instead of spokes, the wheels had discs to reduce their weight and keep their rigidity and strength.

Boiler
Superheated steam passed twice through the boiler to make it extra hot.

Baker valve gear
A system of rods and bell cranks that replaced the Walschaert's valve gear on many modern American steam locomotives.

Cylinders
The 22in. (57cm) diameter cylinders had a 29in. (74cm) stroke.

The "Hudson" Class J-3a 4-6-4 locomotive that pulled the Twentieth Century Limited weighed 166 tons. Ten streamlined engines of this class were built by Alco for the New York Central in 1938. They were capable of hauling the 1,000-ton train at more than 100mph (160kph).

NEW YORK CENTRAL

5445

Streamlined stainless steel cars

Silver and blue livery

EXECUTIVE SERVICES

In the club and baggage car of the Twentieth Century Limited was a barber shop. The train's services also included a valet, the loan of an electric shaver or dictaphone, shoeshining, and complimentary newspapers.

Mallard

" There were no teething troubles with these engines – the finest possible tribute not only to Gresley's overriding direction, but to the detail design, to the workmanship and to the handling of the engine on the road."
O. S. Nock, *Sir Nigel Gresley*

Direction of travel

WORLD SPEED RECORD

On Stoke Bank in the United Kingdom on July 3, 1938, the LNER's locomotive *Mallard* reached 126 miles (202.7 kilometers) per hour) – the unbeaten record for a steam locomotive. A plaque with the record was mounted on the engine. *Mallard* is now on display in the National Railway Museum at York.

Mallard was a record-breaking steam locomotive run by the London and North Eastern Railway (LNER). It was one of 34 Class A4 4-6-2 locomotives used from 1935 to haul express trains between London and Edinburgh. They were designed by Sir Nigel Gresley, chief mechanical engineer of the LNER. Famed for their speed, these streamlined locomotives were based on the Great Northern 4-6-2s designed by Gresley, and they became his best-known achievement. One named *Silver Link* reached a record speed of 112 miles (181 kilometers) per hour just before the famous *Silver Jubilee* express was launched in September 1935. In 1937, the London, Midland and Scottish Railway set a new record of 113 miles (183 kilometers) per hour using a Coronation class 4-6-2. This spurred the LNER to try to regain the speed record. In July 1938, *Mallard* was fitted with a double chimney and coupled to a special test train that had a dynamometer car to monitor its speed. As *Mallard* sped south from Grantham, the driver gave it maximum steam all the way to Stoke summit. Then, as *Mallard* raced downhill, its speed rose to a world steam record of 126 miles (202.7 kilometers) per hour.

COLLECTING WATER AT HIGH SPEED

Because long-distance steam engines used a lot of water, water troughs were placed on main lines. Invented by John Ramsbottom, they were first used in 1860 by the London and North West Railway in North Wales. As each train sped over the troughs, an automatic scoop fitted under its tender was lowered to collect hundreds of gallons of water in a few seconds.

THE DRIVER

With his hand on the regulator, the driver is watching out for the next signal along the line. Drivers of locomotives like *Mallard* were responsible for the safety of hundreds of passengers. Unlike the drivers of modern trains, they had to do most tasks manually. They did not have fail-safe braking systems, or computer-controlled signals that could stop the train if the driver did not respond correctly in time.

THE CORONATION STREAMLINER

The Coronation was a 4-6-2 train that ran at high speeds between London and Edinburgh on the London, Midland and Scottish line from 1937. It had two-tone blue coaches hauled by locomotives with matching livery. Its open-plan design enabled passengers to be served with meals. In the summer months, for a small extra fee, first-class passengers could sit in a beaver-tail viewing car with large windows and armchairs to view the scenery.

CORONATION   1719

[PRO]BLEMS WITH [STREAM]LINING

[In the 19]30s, many railroads around the world [added p]anels to their express trains to make [them stre]amlined. The panels looked sleek but [had to be] removed when the train was cleaned [and repai]red. The fireman of *Mallard* had to [remove t]wo panels before he could clear out [the cin]ders in the smokebox.

Whistle
All engines in this class had American chime whistles.

Double chimney
Enabled exhaust steam and smoke to exit more efficiently.

Boiler
Had a record output of 40,000lb. (18,144kg) of steam per hour.

Streamlined panels
Deflected smoke and soot away from the driver's cab.

External cylinders
Measured 16in. (41.9cm) by 28in. (71.1cm).

Driving wheels
Partially covered by streamlined panels.

Mallard weighed 165 tons and was 70ft. (21.6m) long. It had three cylinders and six driving wheels, which were 6ft. 8in. (2.03m) in diameter. Its eight-wheel corridor tender carried 5,000 gallons (18,925 liters) of water as well as eight tons of coal. The internal mechanical design was also streamlined.

Handrail

Nameplate

Streamlined nose

Signal lamp

MALLARD

N° 4468

Buffer

Gun train

"We will flatten them [the Russians] like a hailstorm."
Adolf Hitler, ordering an
attack on Russia in 1941

Schwere Gustav (or "Heavy Gustav") was the name given to the biggest gun ever built. Before World War 2 (1939–1945), Adolf Hitler decided to have the gun made to smash the huge concrete defenses on the French Maginot Line. *Gustav* was designed to run on specially made double tracks. Its size made it difficult to manufacture, and by the time it was finished by the German firm Krupp in 1941, it was too late for it to be used against France.

Of the two guns finally made, only *Gustav* was used; in 1942 it was fired during the German siege of Sevastopol, a fortified Russian port. Four long trains were needed to transport the parts of the gun from Germany to the siege. It took 1,500 men a month to assemble it. Then 500 men were needed to operate it and to protect it with antiaircraft weapons and spotter planes. Its giant shells could be fired only once every 15 minutes, but they could hit targets almost 30 miles (48 kilometers) away. Although only 48 shells were fired, they destroyed Sevastopol's concrete defenses. (The people of Sevastopol had plenty of time to take cover underground while *Gustav* was put together!) After the Germans captured Sevastopol, *Gustav* was taken apart. Rather than let the weapon fall into Allied hands at the end of the war, the Germans bombed its carrying cars to destroy it.

GUSTAV'S SHELLS

Two types of shell were fired from *Gustav's* 31.5-inch (81-centimeter) barrel: A shell weighing 10,526 pounds (4,763 kilograms), and a 15-foot (4.63-meter) shell weighing over 15,500 pounds (7,030 kilograms), which could pierce concrete. The charges (on the right) were kept separately.

Barrel

A JEEP ON RAILS

When the U.S. army was advancing through Europe in 1944, some of their Willys jeeps were fitted with flanged wheels so they could travel on railroad lines. This meant they could bypass roads that were damaged or clogged with traffic.

Double tracks

TROOP AND ARMORED TRAINS OF WORLD WAR 1

During World War 1 (1914–1918), railroads were used to carry troops and supplies to battle fronts. Many railroad bridges, stations and tunnels were attacked and destroyed. German troop trains (1) transported soldiers long distances to the Russian front. The French troop train (2) had wagons, each carrying 40 soldiers, and flat trucks bearing guns and horse-drawn vehicles. The first British armored trains (3) had guns taken from old ships and were used to defend the coastline.

TRAVERSING THE GUN

Gustav ran on a sheltered double track, 0.75 miles (1.2 kilometers) long. The track was curved so that the barrel could be moved to different angles (traversed) to fire in different directions. The barrel itself could not move very much, so the whole gun was moved back and forth along the track according to where the target was.

Electric hoists
Shells and charges were hauled up to the loading deck one at a time.

Hydraulic rammer
For ramming the projectile and charge accurately.

Loading deck
A round took at least 15 minutes to load.

Barrel
28.9m long, firing shells more than 4m long.

Cradle
Specially built to support the enormous weight.

Generator
Provided power for ammunition hoists and for all lights and electric equipment.

Diesel engine
Each engine provided 1,000hp.

Control room
Where a German colonel commanded the full crew of 500.

Gustav was a massive weapon. Its total weight was 1,329 tons (1,349,970kg). Its barrel was 95ft. (29m) long and had a bore of 31.5in. (81cm). The barrel could tilt upward to 65 degrees, and could fire a giant shell a distance of nearly 30mi. (48km).

Recoil cylinder

Shell loading deck

Crane

DESTROYING ENEMY RAIL LINES

Because of their importance during World War 2, the railroads of Germany and occupied France were bombed by Allied air forces. The main targets were locomotive yards, sheds and works, plus junctions, stations, bridges and tunnels. Damaging the railroad network helped to slow down the movement of goods and supplies to the German army.

Big Boy

" The type got its name when someone at Alco chalked 'Big Boy' on the smokebox of one under construction."
George H. Drury, *Guide to North American Steam Locomotives*

Big Boy was the nickname given to the biggest and strongest steam locomotives ever made. The 25 articulated 4-8-8-4 steam locomotives were built between 1941 and 1944 by the Union Pacific Railroad at the Schenectady Works belonging to Alco. Big Boys were huge: They weighed 534 tons and were 16 feet (4.88 meters) high and 132 feet 9 inches (40.5 meters) long. The earliest locomotive would have fitted twice into Big Boy's tender, and Big Boy's coal-burning grate alone was almost 17 square yards (14 square meters). These giant locomotives were designed to haul 70-car freight trains, weighing 3,000 tons, over the Rocky Mountains. During World War 2 they were used as troop trains, hauling in pairs to transport heavy goods and soldiers across the country to the West Coast. Building up 7,000 horsepower, they would speed along at up to 70 miles (129 kilometers) per hour, eating up 10 tons of coal and more than 650 gallons (2,500 liters) of water in an hour. They were replaced by diesel locomotives in 1962, but several of them can still be seen in railroad museums.

Rocket 0-2-2 (1829) UK:
Length 21ft. 6in.; cylinder diameter 8in.
Tractive effort 900lb.

Lord of the Isles 4-2-2 (1851) UK:
Length 45ft.; cylinder diameter 18in.
Tractive effort 7,000lb.

Mallard 4-6-2 (1935) UK:
Length 71ft.; cylinder diameter 18.5in.
Tractive effort 35,455lb.

Challenger 4-6-6-4 (1936) USA:
Length 125ft.; cylinder diameter 23in.
Tractive effort 57,238lb.

Big Boy 4-8-8-4 (1941) USA:
Length 132ft. 9in.; cylinder diameter 23in.
Tractive effort 74,323lb.

PULLING POWER

From *Rocket* to Big Boy, steam locomotives became bigger and more powerful with every model. It is difficult to compare this power because an engine's performance varies with weather and other conditions. A train that can pull a 3,000-ton load on a level track may only be able to pull 2,000 tons up a hill. For this reason, power is usually measured as tractive effort – the force exerted by a locomotive at the driving wheels.

THE UNION PACIFIC RAILROAD

In 1869, the first trans-American railroad was formed when the Union Pacific Railroad linked with the Central Pacific at Promontory Point in Utah. By 1900 the Union Pacific's main lines went from Ogden, Utah, to Council Bluffs, Iowa, and from Denver, Colorado, to Kansas City, Missouri. Huge locomotives hauled heavy freight trains over the mountains.

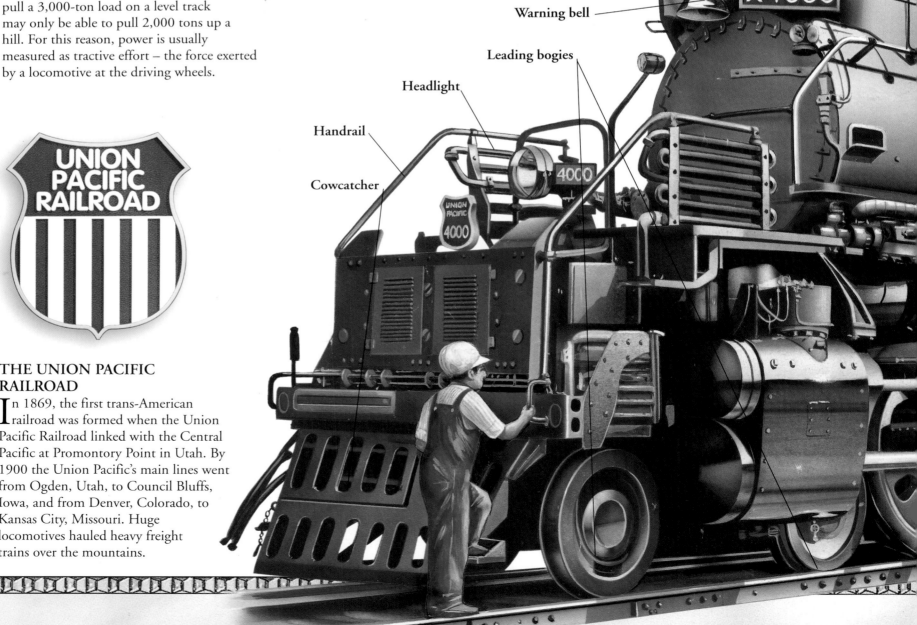

Warning bell

Leading bogies

Headlight

Handrail

Cowcatcher

X4000

GOING AROUND THE BEND

Long steam locomotives had to be articulated so they could go around curves. Including its tender, Big Boy had 38 wheels arranged in six sections. Four of these were pivoted. The two sets of driving wheels were driven by separate sets of cylinders powered by a large boiler.

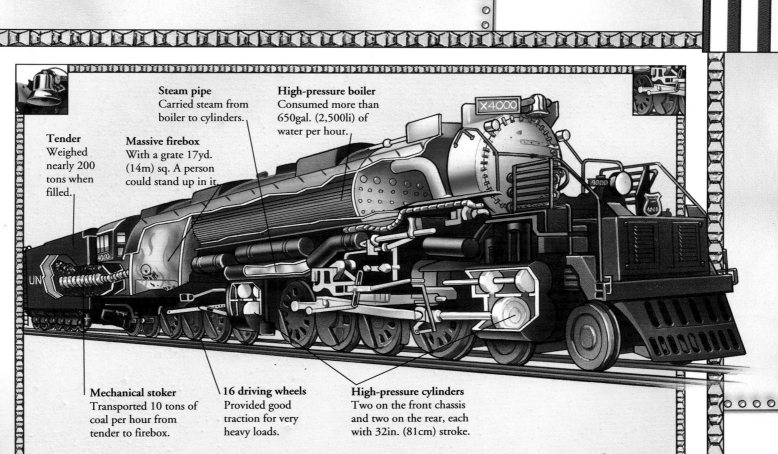

Steam pipe
Carried steam from boiler to cylinders.

High-pressure boiler
Consumed more than 650gal. (2,500li) of water per hour.

Tender
Weighed nearly 200 tons when filled.

Massive firebox
With a grate 17yd. (14m) sq. A person could stand up in it.

Mechanical stoker
Transported 10 tons of coal per hour from tender to firebox.

16 driving wheels
Provided good traction for very heavy loads.

High-pressure cylinders
Two on the front chassis and two on the rear, each with 32in. (81cm) stroke.

Everything about Big Boy was oversized. With its tender, it weighed 534 tons and was 132ft. 9 in. (40.5m) long. With a tractive effort of up to 61 tons, it was able to haul trains weighing more than 3,000 tons at 70mph (129kph). Four high-pressure cylinders powered 16 driving wheels. The 14-wheel tender held 20,668 gallons (79,493 liters) of water and 28 tons of coal. The coal was fed into the massive firebox by a mechanical stoker.

TURNING AROUND

At the end of each journey, steam locomotives with tenders had to be turned 180 degrees. This was done on a turntable in the middle of a special round building. The turntable consisted of a piece of track on a pivot in a circular pit. It was powered by electricity or by steam from a locomotive. The world's longest turntable (135 feet; 41 meters) was built in the United States for Big Boy.

Two sets of eight driving wheels

Trailing bogie

Settebello

ITALY

"The Settebello is named for an Italian card game, the Lucky Seven. The driving controls are located in an upper flight deck, above the lounge, exactly in the style of the first class section in the jumbo jet airliner – but the arrangement was used in the Settebello first."

O. S. Nock, *World Atlas of Railways*

Settebello was a high-speed luxury train that ran between Rome and Milan on the Italian State Railways. It was introduced in 1953 as transportation for business executives in a hurry, and for wealthy tourists who could afford the high price of the tickets – almost double the ordinary first-class fare. Airlines were not yet offering internal shuttle flights, and the Settebello was much faster and more comfortable than any car. At its top running speed of 110 miles (180 kilometers) per hour, it was like a very fast five-star hotel on wheels. Up to 190 passengers sat in 15 spacious first-class lounges with full-size armchairs and sofas. The lounges were very quiet and restful, because the coaches had been completely soundproofed. There were showers on board, and the whole train was air-conditioned. The interior was elegantly decorated, and the exterior was painted in silver-gray and green.

The 391-mile (630-kilometer) journey from Milan to Rome took five and a half hours. Settebello shared the high-speed *Direttissima* (most direct) line with another express train to Rome that left only seven minutes later, but Settebello stayed well ahead. The line traveled through the Appennine Mountains and ran through 18 miles (29 kilometers) of tunnels, including the 11.5-mile (18.5-kilometer) Galleria del Appenino, the world's second-longest main line tunnel. Settebello remained in service until the 1970s.

Milan
Bologna
Florence
Rome

SETTEBELLO AND THE DIRETTISSIMA

Settebello provided a luxury high-speed service between Milan and Rome. It traveled on the *Direttissima* line, which opened in 1934 and passes directly through the Appennine Mountains. The train stopped at Bologna and Florence on the way.

Adjustable window blinds

LUCKY SEVEN

Settebello got its name from an Italian card game, Il Settebello, or "The Lucky Seven." This was because Settebello had seven cars: two power units in front, three cars in the middle, and another two units at the back. This meant that the train did not need separate locomotives at each end, and it would not have to change direction at the terminus in Florence.

FIRST-CLASS TRAVEL

Settebello was a luxury train. Only first-class passengers used its services. All seats were reserved and passengers were seated by a conductor. The train's center car had a spotless electric kitchen and an office for the two attendants. Next door was an elegant restaurant. Italian meals were provided by the Wagons-Lits Company, which ran the world-famous Orient-Express.

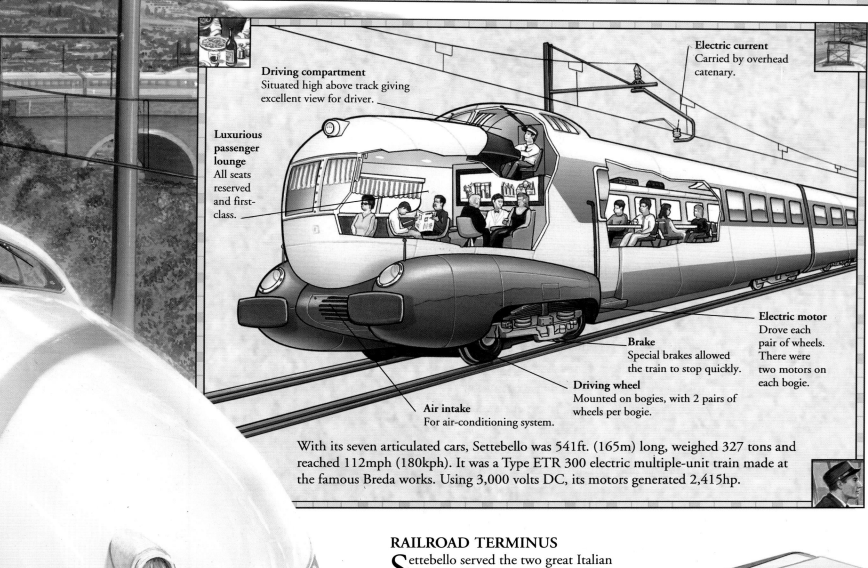

Driving compartment
Situated high above track giving excellent view for driver.

Electric current
Carried by overhead catenary.

Luxurious passenger lounge
All seats reserved and first-class.

Electric motor
Drove each pair of wheels. There were two motors on each bogie.

Brake
Special brakes allowed the train to stop quickly.

Air intake
For air-conditioning system.

Driving wheel
Mounted on bogies, with 2 pairs of wheels per bogie.

With its seven articulated cars, Settebello was 541ft. (165m) long, weighed 327 tons and reached 112mph (180kph). It was a Type ETR 300 electric multiple-unit train made at the famous Breda works. Using 3,000 volts DC, its motors generated 2,415hp.

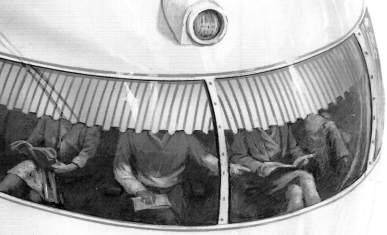

Headlight

Buffer

RAILROAD TERMINUS

Settebello served the two great Italian cities of Rome and Milan. The railroad terminus at Rome (shown on the right) was built in the 1960s. Its modern design, using steel and glass, made the inside seem spacious and full of light – more like a new airport than an old-fashioned train station. The station matched the modern appearance of its most famous train.

THE VIEW FROM THE CAB

The driver's cab on Settebello was set 12 feet (3.66) meters above the track, above and behind the observation lounge. It gave the driver a full view of the line ahead. With a control panel in front of two seats, the cab was like a jet cockpit. The driver could maintain high speeds on the specially constructed line.

West Coast Postal

"This is the night mail crossing the border,
Bringing the cheque and the postal order,
Pulling up Beattock, a steady climb –
The gradient's against her but she's on time."
W. H. Auden, "Night Mail"

The West Coast Postal is one of the busiest British Traveling Post Office trains. It has run nightly from London to Scotland for over 100 years. It has no passengers, but post office staff travel on the train to sort mail for hundreds of destinations.

In the 1950s, the train, as shown here, consisting of up to 14 specially built mail and sorting coaches, left London Euston Station, usually hauled by a powerful Coronation class locomotive, at 8:30 p.m., arriving at Aberdeen at 8:15 the next morning. On its long journey north the West Coast Postal would stop to put down and pick up mail at main railway stations on the West Coast main line. A feature of this train was the mailbag transfer coach where mail could be picked up and set down automatically while the train was traveling at speed. The West Coast Postal train still runs, but its mail-exchange apparatus was last used for exchanging mail bags in 1971.

SUSPENDING THE MAIL

Heavy leather pouches, each containing 30 pounds (13.6 kilograms) of mail from the local sorting office for collection, were suspended at night from special trackside apparatus by post office staff at more than 20 strategic points along the route.

Aberdeen:
8:15 a.m.

London Euston:
8:30 p.m.

ROUTE OF THE WEST COAST POSTAL

The West Coast Postal departs every night from London Euston, stopping to transfer mail at Rugby, Tamworth, Crewe, Preston, Carlisle, Stirling and Perth, before arriving in Aberdeen the next morning. Parts of the train also go to Glasgow and Edinburgh.

PICKING UP THE MAIL

As the train traveled through the night at speeds of up to 62 miles (100 kilometer) per hour, a net was lowered from the side of the mailbag transfer coach. An alarm bell rang to warn the post office staff as the net scooped the suspended leather pouches from the trackside apparatus and they arrived with a loud bang in the sorting coach. The mail in the pouches was then sorted for delivery at stations farther down the line.

Cylinder

MAILBOXES IN MAIL COACHES

At stations, the public could drop a letter directly into a mailbox situated in the side of a Traveling Post Office coach. An extra stamp had to be fixed to the letter to cover the cost of late collection.

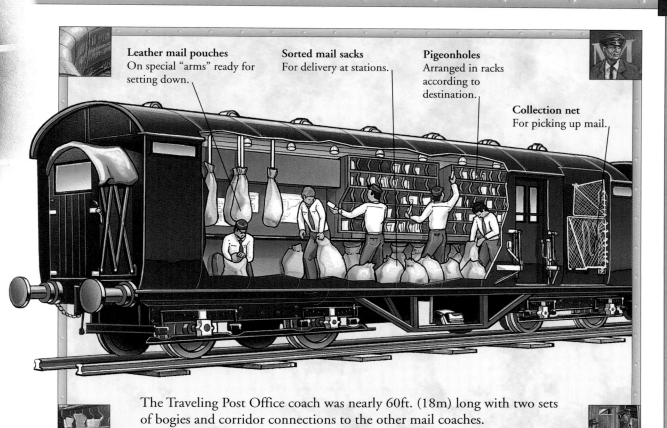

Leather mail pouches
On special "arms" ready for setting down.

Sorted mail sacks
For delivery at stations.

Pigeonholes
Arranged in racks according to destination.

Collection net
For picking up mail.

The Traveling Post Office coach was nearly 60ft. (18m) long with two sets of bogies and corridor connections to the other mail coaches.

Chimney

SORTING THE MAIL

Each Traveling Post Office sorting coach was a hive of activity. Ten post office workers quickly sorted mail into a large rack of destination pigeonholes. Sorted mail was then placed in mail sacks, each with the name of its own district, hanging behind them ready for delivery at the next station, or put into leather pouches for setting down mail while on the move.

Smokebox

Smoke deflector

TRANSFERRING MAIL AT STATIONS

Mailbags from local sorting offices were delivered to the Traveling Post Office train at stations along the line. As the train was scheduled to stop for only a few minutes, staff had to work fast to load the bags into the coaches. At the same time, sorted mail from the train was taken off and loaded onto post office vans. Mail for other destinations was also transferred between trains at certain stations.

Buffer

Puffing Billy

"Only the efforts of a small but determined band of local citizens stand between Puffing Billy and an ignominious retirement."
The Age (Victoria, Australia), March 26, 1954

The much-loved Puffing Billy Railway in Australia is an 8-mile (13-kilometer) section of a 30-inch (76.2-centimeter) narrow-gauge line built outside Melbourne in 1900 by Victorian Railways. Set in the scenic Dandenong Mountains, it ran a rural route from Upper Fern Tree Gully to Gemsbrook, passing through Belgrave and Lakeside. Its purpose was to serve the growing village settlements, taking their fruit crops to Melbourne, and timber from nearby forests. Fitted with "cowcatchers," the two tank locomotives first used on the line were built by Baldwin Locomotives Works in Philadelphia (U.S.A.). Tourists enjoyed the railroad, but it was closed in 1953 after part of it was destroyed by a landslide. In 1958, the section from Upper Fern Tree Gully to Belgrave was rebuilt as a broad-gauge electric railroad linking with Melbourne. In 1954, the Puffing Billy Preservation Society was formed to try to reopen the narrow-gauge railroad from Belgrave to Lakeside. The first section was opened in 1964. The Puffing Billy Railway uses original locomotives that have been restored. The trains are made up of observation cars and open-sided carriages. Volunteers are now restoring another 6 miles (10 kilometers) of track.

STEAM GAUGE

The steam pressure gauge used on Puffing Billy is one of the original instruments, restored and in full working order. The engineer keeps an eye on it as he feeds coal to the firebox and water to the boiler.

AUSTRALIA'S FIRST PRESERVED RAILWAY

Although the Puffing Billy Railway has been owned by the Emerald Tourist Railway Board since 1977, its survival is due partly to the hard work of volunteers, who have been active since 1954. Helped by the army, they have rebuilt stations and relaid the track broken by the landslide, and have restored old steam engines to full working order.

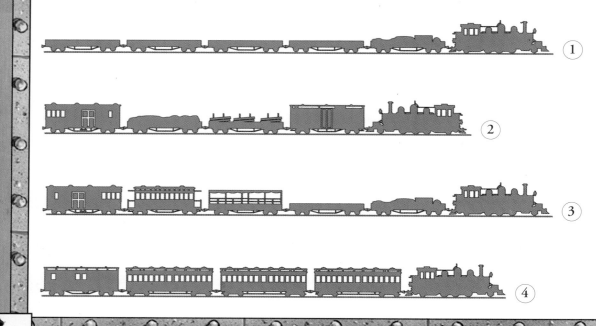

FREIGHT AND PASSENGERS

Several varieties of trains ran on the Puffing Billy Railway: long, open wagons carrying timber cut in the forest (1); goods trains with farm produce such as dairy foods and fruit being taken to markets in Melbourne (2); combined passenger and goods trains, usually with the passenger cars to the rear (combining the trains reduced the cost of running them) (3); tourist trains with open-sided carriages. These were popular for excursions from the city and could carry several hundred passengers in up to eight carriages (4).

AUSTRALIA'S STEAM HERITAGE

Puffing Billy locomotives are 2-6-2 tanks. The first two of these were supplied by the American Baldwin company. After the railroad had been opened, more 2-6-2 tank locomotives were made at the Victorian Railways' workshops in Newport, Australia, and fitted with Westinghouse vacuum brakes. Special wagons were built to carry the locomotives on the broad-gauge network to the narrow-gauge Puffing Billy line.

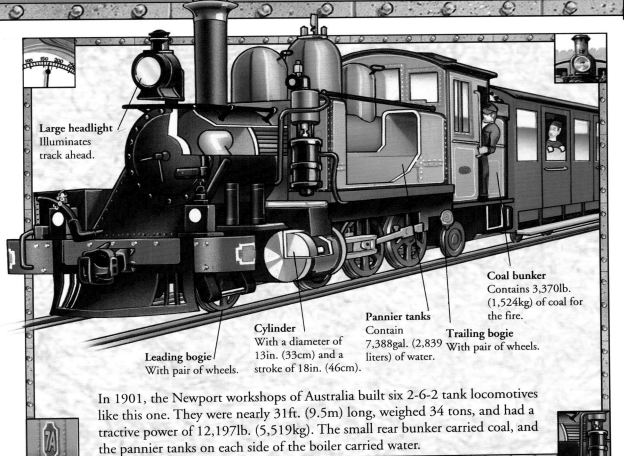

Large headlight Illuminates track ahead.

Leading bogie With pair of wheels.

Cylinder With a diameter of 13in. (33cm) and a stroke of 18in. (46cm).

Pannier tanks Contain 7,388gal. (2,839 liters) of water.

Trailing bogie With pair of wheels.

Coal bunker Contains 3,370lb. (1,524kg) of coal for the fire.

In 1901, the Newport workshops of Australia built six 2-6-2 tank locomotives like this one. They were nearly 31ft. (9.5m) long, weighed 34 tons, and had a tractive power of 12,197lb. (5,519kg). The small rear bunker carried coal, and the pannier tanks on each side of the boiler carried water.

THE END OF THE LINE

The first section of restored track between Belgrave and Lakeside already offers passengers an historic 8-mile (13-kilometer) journey. The remaining 6 miles (10 kilometers) of track from Lakeside through Cockatoo (1) to Gemsbrook (2) is currently being restored.

BUSHFIRE HAZARDS

In February 1926, many bushfires sprang up along the route of the Puffing Billy Railway. Several times as the train rattled its way through the burning hills, passengers stared in terror through the carriage windows at the huge flames trying to swallow up the track.

The Canadian

"The track along the northern shores of Lake Superior was a terrible section to build, cutting a ledge in towering walls of rock rising sheer from the waters of the lake."
O. S. Nock, *World Atlas of Railways*

In 1953, the Canadian Pacific Railway ordered 173 stainless steel cars from the American Budd company to make a new trans-Canadian train called the Canadian. It was launched in 1955 to run daily services between Montreal and Vancouver, and is still in service, mostly for tourists. For most of the journey, the Canadian is hauled by two diesel-electric locomotives of 1,500 horsepower, one with a driver's cab. A third locomotive is added to help the train cross the mountains. The cars are lightweight stainless steel for speed, and painted to match the engine. The train looks very striking as it threads its way through the Canadian Rockies. Seven complete sets of cars are required to run the service. Each train has dining cars, sleeping cars, 60-seat luxury coaches, an observation car, a dome-roofed buffet car with a kitchen, and a car with living quarters for the train's staff.

DRIVING THE CANADIAN

On long-distance North American trains, drivers use a telephone to speak to staff elsewhere on the train, and a radio-telephone link to speak to train controllers. During the Canadian's three-day journey, the crew is changed several times.

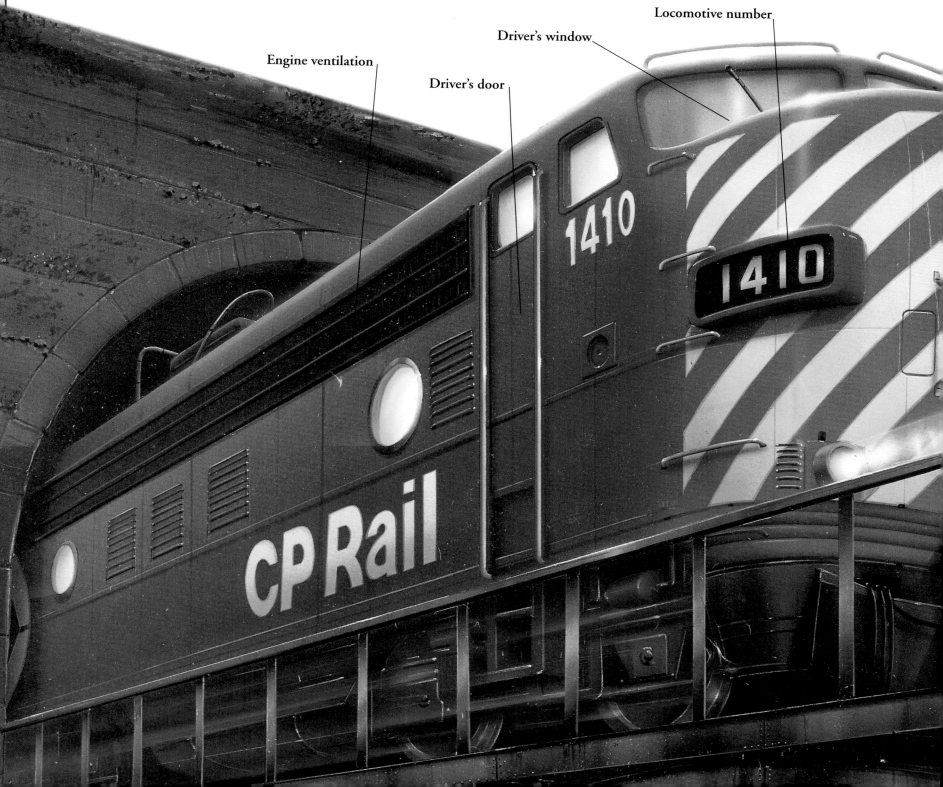

Engine ventilation

Driver's door

Driver's window

Locomotive number

1410

1410

CP Rail

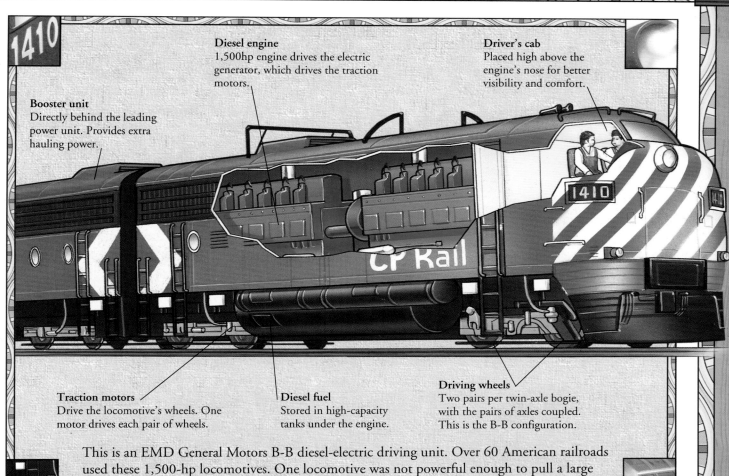

Diesel engine
1,500hp engine drives the electric generator, which drives the traction motors.

Driver's cab
Placed high above the engine's nose for better visibility and comfort.

Booster unit
Directly behind the leading power unit. Provides extra hauling power.

1410

CP Rail

1410

Traction motors
Drive the locomotive's wheels. One motor drives each pair of wheels.

Diesel fuel
Stored in high-capacity tanks under the engine.

Driving wheels
Two pairs per twin-axle bogie, with the pairs of axles coupled. This is the B-B configuration.

This is an EMD General Motors B-B diesel-electric driving unit. Over 60 American railroads used these 1,500-hp locomotives. One locomotive was not powerful enough to pull a large train, so the cab had an equally powerful booster unit attached behind it.

INSIDE THE DOME CAR

The Canadian has a sleek dome car near the front of the train, between its luxury coaches and the dining cars. In the dome car are 26 seats, a buffet and coffee shop, and a bar. A staircase joins the upper and lower levels of the car and allows passengers to walk up to the top of the dome to get a good view during daylight.

THE VIEW FROM THE DOME CAR

The dome car gives passengers good views of the glorious mountain scenery. Early in this century, the Canadian Pacific Railway added an open-top coach to trains passing through the mountains. Hot food and drinks were served to keep passengers warm.

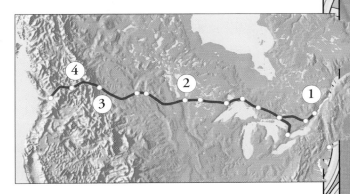

THE ROUTE OF THE CANADIAN

The 2,874-mile (4,636-kilometer) journey from Montreal (1) to Vancouver (4) passes beside Lake Superior before crossing the Great Plains from Winnipeg (2) to Calgary (3). The journey crosses four time zones and takes just over 71 hours – 16 hours less than before.

OBSERVATION CAR

At the very end of the train is another domed observation car, different from the one near the front. Inside the car are three bedrooms, a drawing room, a bar under the dome, and an observation lounge. This is the best part of the train to ride in.

1410

Tube train

"A row of hard faces, immobile,
In the swaying train,
Rush across the flickering background of the fluted dingy tunnel."
Richard Aldington, "In the Tube"

LONDON TRANSPORT'S FAMOUS "ROUNDEL"

The Underground Group, which ran the London Underground, started using the "roundel" symbol in 1908 to make station names stand out from commercial advertising. It was one of the first ever company logos.

TUNNELING THROUGH CLAY

London's tube network was built underground with a machine called the Greathead Shield, invented by James Greathead in 1862. It had huge rotary cutters revolving in the circular cutting edge of the shield, which was forced slowly forward through the clay. Inside the shield, the tunnel wall bolted together from curved sections of cast iron. Modern versions of the shield are driven forward at a rate of more than 300 feet (100 meters) per day.

In 1863, the world's first underground railroad opened in London using steam locomotives. The world's first electric underground train became part of this network in 1890. Earlier underground systems had been built by digging up the street and adding a roof to make a tunnel. This method, called "cut and cover," held up traffic, and sewage pipes got in the way. New parts of London's network were dug much deeper – at 60 feet (18.3 meters), where it went below the Thames River. The work was done inside a metal tube that kept the earth from collapsing into the tunnel as the digging went on. The tunnels, 10.5 feet (3.2 meters) in diameter with cast-iron linings, gave the network the nickname "the Tube." Passengers were carried in windowless coaches. As the network grew, the tunnels got deeper. Some tunnels are 220 feet (67 meters) below ground. Huge ventilator fans provide clean air underground.

Destination panel

Emergency door

Headlight

Driver's cab

BAKER STREET

037

Wedglock mechanical coupler

THE ROUTE OF THE UNDERGROUND

London's underground network now totals 254 miles (410 kilometers), of which 103 miles (167 kilometers) are underground. Extending into the suburbs, 270 stations handle more than 750 million passengers a year.

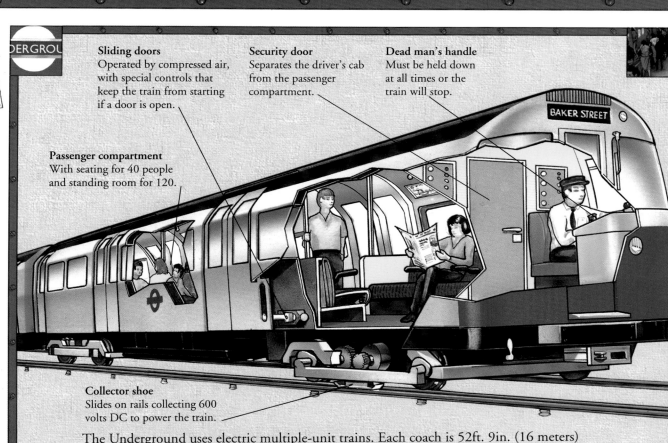

Sliding doors
Operated by compressed air, with special controls that keep the train from starting if a door is open.

Security door
Separates the driver's cab from the passenger compartment.

Dead man's handle
Must be held down at all times or the train will stop.

Passenger compartment
With seating for 40 people and standing room for 120.

Collector shoe
Slides on rails collecting 600 volts DC to power the train.

The Underground uses electric multiple-unit trains. Each coach is 52ft. 9in. (16 meters) long, 8ft. 8 in. (2.6 meters) wide and weighs 28.6 tons. A train with seven coaches has four power cars with four axles each, powered by 300 volt traction motors. The train is almost totally automatic, including braking and accelerating, with combined fail-safe brake systems.

DEEP-LEVEL INTERCHANGE AT PICCADILLY CIRCUS

The Piccadilly and Bakerloo lines form an important interchange station at Piccadilly Circus, London. This complicated underground station took four years to build in the 1920s and was designed to handle over five million passengers a year. Eleven reversible escalators, moving at the rate of 100 feet (30.5 meters) per minute, carry passengers down to the platforms below. The large circular booking hall, 15 feet (4.6 meters) below ground level, covers 15,000 square feet (1,394 square meters). It houses shops, the booking office and automatic ticket machines.

SHELTERING DURING THE BLITZ (1940–1941)

During World War 2, thousands of people in London used the deep-level Tube stations as shelters when German planes bombed the city. Rows of people on folding beds would spend the nights sleeping safely on the station platforms, more than 160 feet (50 meters) below the damaged streets.

Eurostar

"It's sleek to look at silky smooth to travel on and will race between Eropean capitals at three miles a minute. In short the 'Eurostar' is as sensational as it looks."
Peter Semmens, *Railway Magazine*, June 1994

Connecting London to Paris and Brussels, Eurostar is the sleekest, fastest train in daily use in the world. In time it will connect all the main cities of Europe by high-speed rail. Eurostar made history not only for its speed but also for traveling through the new Channel Tunnel under the English Channel between England and France. This huge feat of engineering was carried out by a joint French and British company. The triple-bore tunnel, 31 miles (50 kilometers) long, was opened in May 1994 by the Queen and President François Mitterrand of France. Eurostar itself was built by a team of English, French and Belgian companies. Its design resembles the older French TGV Atlantique. Like the TGV, Eurostar regularly travels at 186 miles (299 kilometers) per hour on the new high-speed lines in France. In Britain and parts of Belgium the train still uses ordinary lines and it goes more slowly. Pneumatic suspension on the coaches gives a smooth ride even at the fastest speeds. Each Eurostar trainset has 18 coaches. No extra coaches may be added to a set. The trainset can be pushed along by the rear power car if the front power car fails. Speed is controlled by computer, and there are three types of brakes to meet safety standards in all three countries.

POWER SUPPLY

Three kinds of power supply are used on Eurostar, two of them picked up overhead by a pantograph on each car. It uses 750 volts in Britain and 3,000 volts in parts of Belgium. On the high-speed lines in France, Belgium and the Channel Tunnel, it draws 25,000 volts from overhead wires. Eventually it will use this everywhere.

LINKS WITH EUROPE

In 1995, Eurostar trains ran only from London (1) to Paris (2) and Brussels (3). New connections are planned for other European cities – Madrid, Milan and Geneva from Paris, and Amsterdam and Frankfurt from Brussels. Eventually, most of Europe will be linked by high-speed rail. Members of the European Union have already agreed to update their rail systems to join the network.

High-intensity headlight

Driver's window

Nose cone

Access panel for electrical equipment

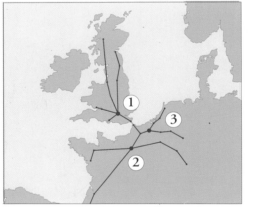

STEPS FOR THREE DIFFERENT LEVELS

The doors of Eurostar trains have electrically operated adjustable steps. Station platforms vary from 36 inches (91.5 centimeters) in Britain to 30 inches (76.0 centimeters) in Belgium and 21.5 inches (55.0 centimeters) in France. The steps can also be lowered so that passengers can reach emergency catwalks in the Channel Tunnel.

AC pantograph
Collects electric current from overhead wire in Tunnel and from high-speed lines in Belgium and France.

Air inlet grilles
Part of the ventilation system.

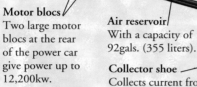

Motor blocs
Two large motor blocs at the rear of the power car give power up to 12,200kw.

Air reservoir
With a capacity of 92gals. (355 liters).

Collector shoe
Collects current from the third rail in the United Kingdom.

Suspension
Coiled-spring secondary suspension.

Eurostar can carry 794 passengers. Fully loaded, it weighs 816 tons. Its traction motors build up 16,400hp, giving a top speed of 186mph (299kph). At this speed it takes one minute five seconds, and a distance of almost 2mi. (3km), to come to a complete stop. A trainset has two power cars and 18 trailer cars, totaling 1,300ft. (394m) in length.

SHUTTLE CAR TRANSPORTER

Freight, lorries and passenger cars travel on Le Shuttle, which runs on the same line as Eurostar. Le Shuttle offers a way to cross the English Channel without having to drive on or off a ferry – and it is not canceled in bad weather. One shuttle train can carry up to 120 cars, 12 coaches, and 1,000 passengers at 85 miles (137 kilometers) per hour. Passengers may stay in their cars for the journey through the Tunnel, which lasts only 35 minutes.

DRIVER'S CONSOLE

The driver's console is in the center of the cab, giving the best view of the track. Computers help the driver control the train. They also read the signals along the line, because the speed of the train often makes them go by in a blur. If the driver does not respond to signals, the train automatically slows down or stops. The console is linked to the control center in France and can check equipment inside the train. Drivers must be able to speak English and French, but they can choose either language to display information on their computers. Speed limits are displayed in miles or kilometers per hour depending on the train's location.

GLOSSARY

Armored train
A train covered in protective metal and carrying guns for use in wartime.

Articulated coach
A coach adjacent to another with a shared bogie.

Articulated locomotive
A steam locomotive with two sets of cylinders, each driving a separate set of wheels, and each set pivoting on its own frame.

Asynchronous
An alternating-current (AC) electric motor whose speed varies with the load, not with the current supplied to it.

Automatic mail collection and delivery
A system for collecting and delivering mail from a moving train.

B-B wheel notation
A description of a diesel or electric locomotive with two twin-axle driving bogies, each pair of axles being driven by one traction motor.

Baker valve gear
A system of valve gears invented by Abner D. Baker in 1903 and modified in 1912 to replace the older Walschaert's valve gear. It used rods and bell cranks instead of link and sliding link blocks, making the gear more efficient and easier to service. Baker valve gear was found mostly on American steam trains built after 1912.

Blast pipe
A vertical pipe fitted beneath the chimney inside the smokebox of a steam locomotive. It carries the exhaust steam from the cylinders and waste material from the fire into the atmosphere. This produces a partial vacuum in the smokebox, which improves the draft for the fire.

Bo-Bo-Bo wheel notation
A description of a diesel or electric locomotive with three twin-axle bogies, with each axle being individually driven.

Bogie
A truck – a frame with wheels – that attaches to the underframe of a wagon, carriage or locomotive and allows it to turn on curved track.

Boiler
The part of a steam locomotive, containing a firebox surrounded by water, that produces steam.

Boiler pressure
The force exerted by the production of steam in the boiler of a steam locomotive.

Broad gauge
Railroad track that is wider than the standard gauge, once used on express lines to allow trains to travel at greater speeds.

Cab
The driver's compartment on a locomotive.

Caboose
The last car at the end of a goods train, often called the guard's van. It has an observation platform at the back.

Carriage
A railroad car that carries passengers.

Carrying wheel
A wheel at the front or back of a bogie, before or after the driving wheels, which supports the engine but is not linked to the power supply by a connecting rod.

Coach
Another name for carriage.

Collector shoe
A metal block on the underside of an electric train that slides along the top of an electrified third rail to collect current.

Compound locomotive
A system for driving steam locomotives using both high pressure and low pressure cylinders. It was pioneered in France by Alfred De Glehn in the late nineteenth century.

Connecting rod
A metal bar that connects the piston rod to the driving wheels of a steam locomotive.

Corridor connection
A short flexible corridor connected between railroad carriages that enables passengers to walk the length of a train.

Corridor tender
A corridor fitted to the inside of a steam locomotive tender that enables the crew to pass between the cab and the rest of the train. It was once used by some rail companies on their long-distance nonstop express trains to allow a fresh crew to take over during the journey.

Cowcatcher
A V-shaped metal frame at the front of a locomotive that pushes obstacles off the track.

Cylinder
An elongated, cylindrical chamber that contains the piston.

Diesel electric
A locomotive powered by the electric current produced by a generator driven by a diesel engine.

Dome car
A passenger coach fitted with a protruding glass roof that gives passengers views of the scenery.

Driving wheel
One of the wheels of a locomotive that is connected to the power supply and makes the locomotive move forward.

Dynamometer car
A carriage fitted with equipment for measuring and recording the horsepower and speed of a locomotive at work.

Electrical induction
The production of an electric current by a change of magnetic field.

Electro-pneumatic brakes
Air-pressure brakes that are activated by electricity.

Firebox
The part of a steam locomotive where coal or logs are burned.

Flanged wheel
A wheel fitted with a projecting inside rim that makes a train stay on the track.

Footplate
The floor in the driver's cab of a steam locomotive where the driver and fireman stood.

Gauge
The distance between the inner faces of the rails of railroad track. This is usually 4 feet 8.5 inches (143.5 centimeters), but nonstandard gauges may be narrower or wider than this.

Gradient
A measurement of a slope or hill, usually expressed as a percentage or a ratio. A gradient of 1 in 50 (up), or 2 percent, means that the slope rises 1 unit in height (either feet or meters) for every 50 units of distance. The closer the ratio or the higher the percentage, the steeper the gradient; 1 in 50 is steep for a main line.

Grate
The part of a steam locomotive firebox that contains the fuel for the fire.

High pressure
The pressure of steam in a boiler of a steam locomotive (always measured in pounds) when it exceeds 200lb per square inch.

Horsepower
A unit of power equal to 33,000 feet per pound per minute (75 kilograms per meter per second), or 746 watts.

Locomotive
The engine unit of a train, which can be disconnected from the rest of the train.

Loop
A railroad track that gains height by turning in a full circle and crossing over itself at a higher level.

Maglev
Magnetic levitation – a way of powering a train using magnetic attraction or repulsion instead of wheels attached to a power supply.

Marshaling yard
An area where railroad goods wagons are sorted and linked up to form complete trains.

Mechanical stoker
A device used in large steam locomotives that conveyed coal from the tender to the firebox.

Multiple unit
A train consisting of two or more powered units coupled together and operated by one driver.

Multitube boiler
A steam boiler in which heat is taken through many tubes to heat the water more effectively.

Narrow gauge
Railroad track that is narrower than standard gauge, often used in difficult terrain.

Navvy
A laborer who worked on canals and railroads.

Observation car
The coach of a passenger train, usually at the rear, that provides large windows for scenic viewing.

Pannier tank
One of two or more tanks on a steam locomotive that carry the water supply in containers on both sides of the boiler.

Pantograph
The spring-loaded and pivoted framework that links the top of an electric locomotive with its overhead power supply line.

Pigeon hole
One of a row of small compartments used for sorting letters in a traveling post-office train.

Power car
A car that contains an electric train's power supply. It is the equivalent of the engine, although it may propel the train from either end. Electric trains often have two power cars, one at each end.

Pullman car
A type of luxury car invented in 1859 by George Pullman in America. It was the world's first sleeper car.

Radio telephone
A telephone system that works by using radio waves instead of fixed transmission wires.

Regenerative brakes
A braking system used on DC electric locomotives in which the traction motors work as generators and put energy back into the supply system.

Regulator
The valve on a steam locomotive that controls the amount of steam passing from the boiler to the cylinders, thus controlling the speed.

Rheostatic braking
An electrical braking system used on the driving axles of modern high-speed trains. The traction motors act as generators, producing electrical energy that is absorbed by the wheels. This system does not need any outside power supply and so it can be used in emergencies.

Rolling stock
Any railroad car that is not an engine or a power car and cannot propel itself.

Saddle tank
A type of tank on a steam locomotive. It carries the water supply in a large curved container around the top half of the boiler.

Safety valve
A device fitted to the boiler of a steam locomotive that automatically releases excess steam when a certain pressure is reached.

Sanding gear
A device fitted to locomotives that drops sand onto the rails to prevent the wheels slipping.

Self-propelled
A vehicle, such as a railroad gun or crane, that contains its own power unit enabling it to move.

Signal
A warning device at the side of the track to control the safe movement of trains. A combination of mechanical arms and/or colored lights are used and controlled from a central signal box.

Sleeper (tie)
A beam made of timber, steel or concrete that holds the rails to the correct gauge and distributes the load of the train to the ballast below.

Smokebox
The front section of a steam locomotive's boiler that contains the steam pipes to the cylinders, the blast pipe and the chimney.

Spark arrester
A metal mesh that is fitted to the top of a steam locomotive's chimney to prevent the emission of hot coals and sparks.

Spike
A heavy square section nail that holds the rail to the sleeper.

Streamlining
A specially designed smooth shape applied to locomotives and coaches to reduce wind resistance when traveling at high speed. Streamlined trains became popular in the 1930s. Some of the same principles were applied to the modern aerodynamic designs of high-speed trains such as the Shinkansen, TGV and *Eurostar*.

Stroke
A measurement of the distance that a piston travels when it moves up and down.

Superelevated
A curved two-rail track with one rail raised above the level of the other rail, enabling trains to tilt and to move safely at high speeds.

Switchback
A section of track that enables trains to zigzag up the side of a steep slope by alternately driving into a dead end and then backing out and up.

Tender
A car connected to the engine of a steam locomotive that carries the fuel and water supply.

Third rail
An extra rail alongside the two running rails that carries electric current to an electric train. It is an alternative to the pantograph.

Traction motor
A motor that makes wheels turn when they are supplied with electric power.

Tractive effort
A measurement of the force exerted by a locomotive at its driving wheels. This is the standard way of measuring a locomotive's power, because performance varies so much with weather and track conditions, the size of the load, the gradient, and other factors.

Traductor arm
A movable metal arm, used on traveling post-office trains, that suspended mail bags for delivery while the train was moving.

Train
A series of vehicles on flanged wheels, pulled along a track by an engine or power car.

Transformer
A device that changes the voltage of an electric current without changing its frequency.

Traverse
A curved section of railroad track that enables a rail-mounted gun barrel to be moved horizontally.

Valve
A device that moves to create an opening to let steam, water or gas in or out.

Wagon
A railroad car that carries freight.

Walschaert's valve gear
A device that controls the distribution of steam in the steam chest of a locomotive cylinder. It was invented by a Belgian railroad engineer, Egide Walschaert, in 1844 and subsequently used by many railroads around the world.

Water scoop
A mechanical device that was lowered from a steam locomotive tender to collect water from troughs while the train was moving fast.

Water trough
A long metal channel, containing water and positioned centrally between the railroad track, that enabled steam locomotives to collect water while traveling at high speed.

Westinghouse vacuum brake
An automatic braking system operated by atmospheric air pressure. The vacuum brake was invented by an American engineer, George Westinghouse, in 1871.

Wheel arrangement
The way in which the driving wheels and carrying wheels are positioned on the bogies of a steam locomotive. Engineers kept changing the numbers and kinds of wheels on locomotives to try to achieve maximum performance, so there is no standard number or order of wheels. The most common way of describing wheel arrangement is the Whyte system, invented in 1900. In this system, the wheels are numbered in pairs from the front of the train, two on each side, so that 4-4-2 means 4 carrying wheels, 4 driving wheels, and 2 more carrying wheels. The carrying wheels may also be called leading and trailing wheels. 2-6-0 means 2 leading wheels, 6 driving wheels and no trailing wheels behind the driving wheels. Wheel arrangement is characteristic of particular classes of trains; for example, a popular arrangement in the 1930s was the 4-6-2 or "Pacific" arrangement. Diesel and electric locomotives have different notation systems. Bo-Bo is a diesel configuration of two sets of 4-wheel bogies with each axle being individually driven. The letters denote driving axles, so that A is 1, B is 2, C is 3; and axles individually driven are designated "0".

Wheelbase
The distance between the outer driving wheels of a locomotive, measured from the point at which the wheels make contact with the rails. A locomotive with a short wheelbase (for example, a 0-4-0) is able to travel around sharper bends than a locomotive with a long wheelbase (such as a 4-8-4). Pivoting unpowered bogies, or trucks, are positioned at the front and rear of locomotives to help long engines to travel around curves.

INDEX

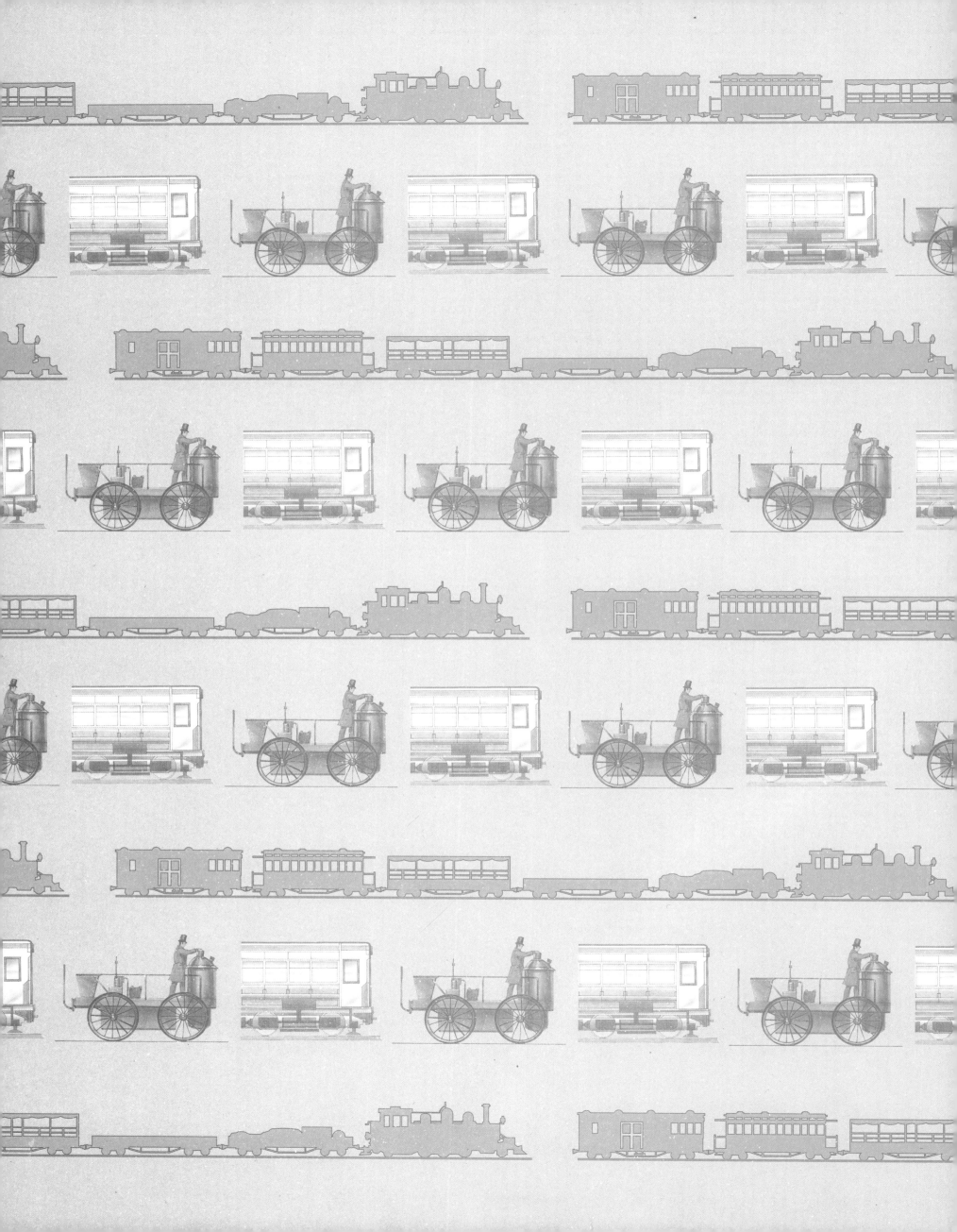